FOCUS ON FAMILY LIFE

GLADYS M. HUNT

Contemporary
Discussion Series

Baker Book House
Grand Rapids, Michigan 49506

Standard Book Number ISBN: 0-8010-4001-9

Library of Congress Catalog Card Number: 74-124568

Copyright © 1970
by Gladys M. Hunt

Printed in the
United States of America by
Malloy Lithographing, Inc.
Ann Arbor, Michigan

First Printing, June 1970
Second Printing, July 1971
Third Printing, April 1974

How to Use the Book

THIS BOOK IS DESIGNED for adult discussion groups interested in exploring family life.

Plan on a minimum of an hour, preferably more, to handle each chapter and the questions which follow. A superficial treatment of the material will only frustrate group members.

Read the assigned chapter. Because of the time factor, most groups will want members to read the chapter before the group meeting. However, in the event that this is not done (1) chapters could be read aloud, or (2) sections could be assigned to small groups for silent reading, followed by a summary of their assignment.

The value of the discussion will hinge on the group's grasp of the chapter being considered.

The discussion leader must prepare ahead of time. Ten questions follow each chapter. Their value will depend on each group's needs and interests. Few discussions will allow time to use all ten questions. The leader must choose the series of questions he considers most valuable for his group discussion. Be alert to guard against superficial answers and pursue the issue with further questions of your own.

In using questions that have more than one part, do not throw out for group discussion more than one part of the question at a time.

A good discussion involves all the members. Discourage those who overparticipate by asking those who have not yet participated for their opinions. However, be careful to treat personal individuality with integrity.

Discussion patterns should flow between members of the group, not just from leader to participant. The discussion leader is only a guide to stimulate discussion among group members and to keep the sharing on target, in view of both subject and time.

The ideal discussion pattern looks like this:

not like this:

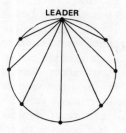

Happy learning together!

Introduction

PICK UP ALMOST ANY PERIODICAL on the newsstand today and you'll find articles raising doubts about the family's ability to withstand the onslaught of fast living, secularism, and changing values. Some go so far as to question the validity of family life as we have known it, with articles bearing such titles as: *Is Marriage Outmoded? Can the Family Survive? The Disappearance of the Old Morality.*

It's time to raise another voice — a different voice — reaffirming the family and pointing to a biblical view of family relationships. It's time to stir up Christians to the quality of living God had in mind when He designed the family.

These eight chapters are intended to stimulate fresh thinking on family relationships and responsibility. At the end of each chapter are discussion questions to guide the group in sharing insights and experiences, as the members learn together. *Focus on Family Life* is a springboard for meaningful discussion and more biblical family life.

Table of Contents

The Family 1
Is God's Idea

No INSTITUTION is under greater attack today than *the family*. Yet no unit is more vital to the existence of meaningful society than the family. The family, the home, is the basis of societal structure because God planned it that way.

The Old Testament is full of *family* emphasis. God dealt with families. He gave instructions for family life. He gave promises to the family. He constructed the family in the very beginning by creating male *and* female in such a way that they could express their oneness and love physically so that each might contribute to the conception of offspring. God could have made people any way He chose. He chose the marvel of our present design; He allows the child to grow in the womb of the mother, to be nourished and cared for by the mother and father. He provides the security of oneness within the family so that wholeness of character and personality can develop within the safety of a home. No offspring in all of creation has so long a period of training, developing, and family care as children.

ONENESS VS. TOGETHERNESS

That's why *oneness* is so important a concept in Scripture. God created man, Adam, and gave him the task of naming the creatures He had made. Picture Adam studying the anatomical characteristics of each animal, considering how certain creatures fit into species, giving them names which would identify them in God's creation. But for Adam, the Bible says, there was not found a helper fit for him. When God created the woman, so specially designed to meet the total needs of that total man, Adam immediately recognized that she was *his kind* and said, "This at last is bone of my bones and flesh of my flesh." In that declaration Adam recognizes God's idea of oneness.

Genesis 2:24 immediately follows with a verse which is repeated by both Jesus and Paul in their discussion of marriage and moral responsibility. "Therefore a man leaves his father and his mother and cleaves to his wife, and they become one flesh."

This single verse, by virtue of its content and its repetition in Scripture, teaches us more about the home and the family than any other single verse. The establishment of a new home involves a break with former close attachment to parents, and involves the *cleaving* (what a strong word!) of the man to his wife. The necessity to *cleave* or to *cling* together implies that this is to be worked at in daily life in such a way that the end product is *oneness*.

Secular marriage counselors speak of togetherness, the idea of a 50-50 relationship. Maybe that's the best some people can manage. But God always talks in terms of *oneness*. Oneness is a large concept because it originates with God, not with man, especially sinful man for whom *meness* comes more naturally. The sweet fruits of oneness are fulfilment, peace and genuine concern for another. There's a safety in oneness because divisiveness is gone.

HOME IS A SAFE PLACE

And a home should be a safe place. It's a place where the whole person receives refreshment and encouragement. It's a place where its members are free from attack. Life may be brutal, full of misunderstandings outside the home, but when family members gather there is mutual encouragement, freedom from attack, understanding, and the nourishment of love.

Psychologists are now saying that a child's character is determined long before he reaches school age. Character speaks of an individual's moral vigor or reliability, his self-discipline, his behavior in matters of right and wrong, his value structure, his stability. Character reflects the inner person. The home is where character is developed and strengthened; and this says something to us about the importance of the first years of a child's life.

Personality is the outward expression of the inner person. Personalities should be free to develop and flourish within the nurture of the family. When family members are secure in the Lord and experience oneness with each other, each is free to be who he is. We should have genuine appreciation for individual differences. Oneness never means sameness. That's sometimes the jarring, unsettling fact of life. But it can also be the joy of family life. Our rigidity or insecurity should not thwart the free development of a child who needs our love and encouragement. By this, I do not mean a permissiveness of behavior when there should be discipline. A fine line exists here, one which parents can trample over without realizing it.

The family provides the child with his first secure relationships so he can begin to act and react as a social being. He learns what is acceptable, what it means to be sensitive to others, what brings joy to himself and others — and a host of attitudes which involve interpersonal relationships. Proper self-esteem is the family's good gift to each of its members.

Self-esteem is necessary for a healthy emotional life. Everyone has to believe in himself a little bit before he is free to believe in anyone else. A person with a low self-image usually has trouble liking anyone else, because he doesn't even like himself. Healthy families give their children healthy concepts of self. The Christian family goes a step further and says: "God loves you. You are valuable to Him." I was pleased when my young nephew, in filling out a third-grade evaluation form, answered the question, "What do you want to be?" with *Myself*. Everyone should like being himself. Oh, not without some wishes for improvement; but basically we should feel comfortable being who we are.

WHAT THE FAMILY OFFERS ITS MEMBERS

Too idealistic, you say? Maybe, but that is what God had in mind when he made the family.

He could have provided human offspring with the ability to grub for food at an early age and to fend for themselves. But man is more than physical. He is also intellectual and spiritual. His whole person needs development, protection, and instruction in the ways of God.

Eric Fromm in his book, *The Art of Loving*,

speaks of parents who provide milk for their children; that is, they provide for the physical needs of their family. But he laments that there are so few who supply milk *and* honey. *Honey* is the ingredient that feeds the inner person, that gives sparkle and significance to life.

Christian parents, more than any others, have the resources to provide the honey of life. When they fail to do this they are missing God's plan for the family to furnish nourishment for the whole person within their home. We are often found bemoaning the degeneration of society, but we do little to redeem the quality of life within our own small society — the family. Society does not disintegrate unless its family life disintegrates. With all the contemporary pressures on the home and family, we need to exercise our discipline, our intellect, our spiritual understanding in reaffirming the importance of family life and uplifting its quality.

This is what it means to train up a child in the way he should go. Sometimes we act as though teaching a child the plan of salvation is the sum total of family training. We all know of homes where biblical doctrine is taught in the abstract and not lived out in life. Spiritually needy mothers and fathers can tear a child's personality apart. If we tell a child often enough that he is worthless, he eventually believes it. If we give love only when a child excels or pleases us, we unwittingly teach a false view of love. If we must always be authoritatively right, we either encourage weak personalities or rebellion. When parents quarrel, when they refuse to understand each other, they provide an environment of intense insecurity which is poor training, to say the least.

The Christian home is the number one example

of God's saving grace. The Christian home, more than the church, demonstrates to the world the difference faith in God makes in human life. The church is made up of families, a corporate group, who bear witness to the same truth. But weak homes mean a weak church. Too often we attempt to shore up a weak church by having extra meetings which only tear the home further apart.

GODLINESS BEGINS AT HOME

The Christian home and the life of the Christian family ought to be open to observation by the world. That is, we should not be ashamed to have others scrutinize our lives. Not that any home would be perfect — because people aren't perfect. But the world ought to be free to look in on Christian family life and observe a group of varied personalities, with varied problems, working them out in a kind of unity and love which validates the redemptive ministry of Christ. The world does, in fact, observe more of our family life than we know — which is part of the problem. And more serious than the world's observation is our own children's observation.

No one is wise enough to answer all family needs in himself. The distinguishing mark of a Christian family is that they know Who does have the answers. How easily we betray the quality of our personal walk with God! The family does need to pray together about the nitty-gritty issues of each day. God is a better attitude-changer than all the family arguments in the world. At the same time, the family without the wisdom of discipline is not obeying biblical instruction. It's praying *and* disciplining. It is asking for wisdom beyond our own. It is personal integrity of life and the unfailing expectation of this in our children. To lay claim to being a Christian family is an awesome responsibility and a great privilege.

The Old Testament has much to say about fathers training their children, about the importance of not marrying unbelievers so that homes will be godly homes. It speaks of parents rehearsing the marvelous works of God so that children's children will hear of the salvation of the Lord. God knew that the way the home went would be the way the Jewish nation went. If we neglect God's basic unit of society we cannot expect all else to go well.

Recently while reading a modern translation of Malachi 2:15 I was struck by words I had never noticed before. The prophet says, "Has not God made you one and sustained for us the spirit of life? And what does he desire? Godly offspring." What a gift to offer God as the fruit of our lives, the fruit of our homes — *godly offspring.* I can think of no treasure more beautiful to offer the Savior.

The verse goes on to say, "So take heed to yourselves and let none be faithless to the wife of his youth. 'For I hate divorce,' says the Lord God of Israel."

That's what the family is all about. It is important to God because through it the children He gives us are molded in godliness. It is a witness to the world of the truth of God's grace. It reflects God's character and concern for men and women who need to know the safety and the freedom of redemptive love.

DISCUSSION QUESTIONS

1. As you review the chapter, what wisdom do you observe in God's plan to make the family the basic unit of society?

2. Define the pressures which put the family under attack in contemporary society.

3. What should the family offer its members? How does this affect both character and personality?

4. What does God's concept of *oneness* offer the family in contrast to *togetherness*? Define what you think should characterize a Christian home.

5. What new insights do you have into the meaning of Genesis 2:24? Observe the added emphasis given the verse in the context of Matthew 19:5; Mark 10:7, 8; I Corinthians 6:16; Ephesians 5:31.

6. Why is self-esteem so important? How does this differ from pride? How can the first be developed without encouraging the second?

7. What do our attitudes and our actions teach our children about God? Give examples.

8. Discuss some areas of life which you think provide *honey* for your family.

9. Why are we often reluctant to have our family life open to the scrutiny of others? How can we be more realistic about the witness of our home? Discuss the difficulty of the minister's family in this regard.

10. Why is the family so important to God? In what ways is it the number one demonstration to the world of God's saving grace?

Wives, Love
Your Husbands **2**

I WAS A ROMANTIC TEEN-AGER when I first came across Paul's words of instruction to Titus that the older women should train the young women to love their husbands (Titus 2:4). I thought this a somewhat ridiculous kind of instruction, for surely a wife *would* love her husband.

How little I understood what love really is! Our cultural pattern forces such an anemic concept of love on us that it is easy to grow up thinking love is only a warm, emotional glow felt in the presence of the beloved.

While love most certainly includes that warm glow, it has many more elements than this. It involves the whole person. We could accurately say: Wives, love your husbands with your emotions. Wives, love your husbands with your will. Wives, love your husbands with your intellect, with your mind. The practical implications are staggering.

This is the involvement of love. But what is *love?* Can it be defined? Probably not adequately, but trying does help our understanding. Someone said, "Love is a principle of life which produces righteousness in another person." Or, love is desiring another's highest good. Clearly, love is not passive, but active. Love is not something that happens to you, but something you positively do.

15

Love is an act of the will. The morning the baby cries, and the four-year-old spills her milk and the diaper pail is overflowing is no time to depend on the emotional feeling of love.

Love involves friendship. It contains a quiet kind of appreciation and affection for another's spirit and intellect. Married love includes a deep desire to belong to another person, to give the right of one's self and to possess the beloved. Love must ultimately reflect something of God's kind of love which keeps on loving even when the worthiness of the person is in question. Married love should include all of these concepts because it involves the merging of two lives.

It is important at the outset to realize that sin has set a tremendous road block in the way of our loving another person. Any hope we have of loving others is found in God. We love because He first loved us. As we experience His love, we are potentially freed from obsession with self. As the life of Christ becomes real in us, we are released to love in a way that pleases Him.

It has been wisely said that most young couples aim at nothing and hit it. We ought to have high goals in mind for those we love. A wife ought to desire the very best God has for her husband. And desiring this, she ought to realize that God expects her to play a major role in bringing about his best. For this is what a helpmeet is: one who is a suitable helper, who answers his inner needs, who constructively understands.

LEADERSHIP IN THE HOME

What is a husband's highest good? Certainly that he fulfill the role God has given him as a husband. God has placed the leadership of the home in the hands of the husband. This is basic to the husband-wife relationship and is seen clearly in passages such as Ephesians 5, I Corinthians 11:3 and I Timothy 3:12, where the husband is declared the head and the wife is instructed to be submissive to his headship.

Emancipated women have chafed at Paul's teaching. I have even heard women speak lightly of Paul's writings, calling him a woman-hater; but their reaction shows that they do not understand. Some women react as if submission means inferiority. Then, as if to prove their superiority, they compete for headship. No one, they have said, is going to take advantage of us!

Submission does not mean inferiority. It does not imply an under-privileged position. It simply means orderliness and responsibility. In Ephesians 5:21 we are all told to be subject to one another out of reverence for Christ. The Bible says very little about rights, but much about responsibility.

God has a plan for a family to live in peace and righteousness, with each member of the family experiencing fulfillment. He made man; He made woman to complement man. He knows how each will find the greatest happiness and completion. So God gives each a role and a responsibility, and says, "This is what I want *you* to do."

This is necessary for survival. Theodore Bovet comments that "headless or two-headed organisms are incapable of life, and marriage is an organism." God has given the man the role of headship and the woman the responsibility to see that he is the head. We have stressed freedom and personal rights so much in our culture that we have almost come to believe the concepts of going 50-50 and togetherness. But the Bible speaks of *oneness* and going all the way.

Personally, I have never met a woman who did not want a man capable of being the "head." Watching families where the wife nags at the husband, it sometimes looks as though, in her frustration at *his* submission, she were goading him to be the head, despising him because he is not. Women who are not willing to carry the responsibility of submission openly declare their discontent to the world. On the other hand, no man ought to get his sense of well-being from degrading another. That misses the biblical point. The husband's job is not to recite this teaching to his wife. His responsibility is so clearly outlined that he has all he can handle if he simply obeys that. Happiness and fulfillment are not found in exploiting rights, but in taking the responsibility God has given.

Today's cultural drift in the wife's role is doubtless the result of the campaigning of Susan Anthony and other feminist crusaders. I always feel a little proud of their courage in opposing the abuses of society. God never meant for anyone to be a second-class citizen, or to be thought unworthy of respect. He makes that quite clear when he says, "In Christ there is neither male nor female, bond nor free. . . ." And it is true that women were often pawns, that they could not vote nor own property, nor gain a divorce under any circumstances. It is true that society had let some men become unreasonable buffoons who bolstered their egos with meaningless commands and absolute authority. Certain changes were in order and came about through the graciousness of God.

The feminist crusade carries on. Equal rights in employment and salary, outrage at exploitation as a sex symbol in advertising, insistence that women be more than "just a housewife" are only part of a vigorous contemporary campaign — a campaign which will necessitate that every Christian woman reevaluate her role in the light of Scripture.

But rights for women are one thing. The responsibility of being a Christian wife is another. Every wife needs periodically to take inventory, checking off whatever activities and attitudes she has collected which keep her from being what God has asked her to be.

It is not always easy for a man to be the head spiritually or in general household leadership. Some men are natural leaders; they easily assume authority and make decisions. But just being born male in gender does not assure that this will be true. Often women react more quickly, have more intuition and speak more fluently. Their seeming *savoir-faire* can so overwhelm a man, generally more realistic about his abilities, that he ends up thinking his wife can do it better anyway!

It is a heavy responsibility to lead a family. It not only means earning a livelihood, but directing in the more encompassing needs of the family as well. God knew best how a wife can help. He says to her: "Let your husband be the head of the home. Help him to be all that I have intended him to be, for then he becomes a man whom I can use in your home, in the community, in his job and in the church." The wife's attitude should tell her husband: "You can do it. I think you're wonderful!" Strangely, she finds her own fulfillment in this role.

In practical terms this might mean that she will not be quite so quick to speak or to pronounce her viewpoints. In a very real sense, she will set up situations in the home in which her husband's headship is encouraged. This is not to help him assume a role of an egotistic kingpin in the home, but to give him her necessary vote of confidence. Today's woman has the wonderful opportunity of playing a good supporting role, because she is generally well-educated, and no longer naive and out of touch with the world the man knows. Husbands look to their wives for help, for opinions, for a fresh outlook; and it is good for the marriage relationship.

It is foolish to be jealous of the one who casts the deciding vote or to think he is necessarily the best, the greatest, the infallible one. No, it is simply his responsibility to make the decision. We see this in the business and government worlds all the time. A good administrator consults his experts and asks advice. A man's wife is often his best expert in matters relating to the family. Yet he must not stand before the world as Adam did, and say, "The woman said this and thus to me. . . ." Today's husband wants to ask his wife, but he must bear the responsibility for the decision.

Loving her husband, a wife never says, even in jest, anything that would injure him. That's part of what Ephesians 5:33 means when it says wives should respect their husbands. There should be no sarcasm, bitterness, or verbal attack before the children, to neighbors, or in front of friends. The wife guards her husband's reputation. Further, she maintains a home which psychologically supports him, which is a fortress against batterings he may receive in the world. There, in the home together, as husband and wife, they are safe from attack. They cleave to each other, for they are joined in purpose, mind, and body.

HIS BEST BEFORE GOD

Loving wives pray for their husbands. That seems a simple statement, but it is so easy for crying babies and a sink full of dishes to keep us from doing the most helpful thing available. A wife need not be embarrassed to mention her husband to God! She longs for him to be a man of faith; for him to sustain daily communication with the Lord and to desire to be more like Him. The husband stands as God's representative to the family and ideally reveals the characteristics of God's Fatherhood to his household.

But praying brings the wife into focus before God, along with her husband; and the shining light of God's presence may reveal personal wrongs that need to be put right so that God can answer prayers. A desire for practical faith and righteousness in the husband demands the same for the wife. Hysterical fears are not an encouragement to faith on the part of a husband, whether the fears are over money or a sick child. Encouraging a husband to keep late hours and stay in bed late in the morning hardly inspires a daily time with God. The wife has a major part in arranging the family life so her husband can meet with God. She is not jealous of God.

A wise wife finds something meaningful to talk about with her husband. Sharing ideas must be a constructive activity, however. Any tendency to pettiness has got to go. It is too easy for women to be bothered by traits or actions of another and to build up, in a series of conversations, false evidence in the husband's mind. There are church leaders who have acted in pettiness only because their wives had colored their thinking with slanted information gained on the telephone. There are men who have acted coolly to associates because of this kind of "discussion." God wants to help Christian wives to be so filled with Himself that this ingredient of life is under His control. A loving wife has a loving attitude towards others.

ON BEING LOVING

Wives need to keep their sense of the romantic. They not only need to keep it, but to cultivate it. The hurried pace of life in our homes makes romantic love difficult. Women are being shaped by the times, someone said, and the shape is no longer feminine, gracious, and loving. For all the pressure of the children's needs, the community projects, and the dirty kitchen floor, the wife still needs to be her husband's lover. She may wonder why her husband's affectionate moments come while she is stirring the gravy; but if her sense of the romantic is squelched by duties and things, she has lost the enjoyment of loving.

It takes such a little touch to keep the extra special feeling of love alive in daily life. It can be "I love U" carved on the top crust of an apple pie, or a note tucked in with a sandwich, or a terse verse on the bathroom mirror or a fresh dress at supper time. Romantic love has come to mean sex in today's world, and sex has often been degraded to hasty acts which are the sum total of many romantic relationships.

There are dozens of tender words, looks of understanding, and special moments in every day that make up genuine love. Wives who love their husbands know that these must not be sacrificed to the day's pressure. Further, Christian wives should not flinch at the concept of being a lover, for this is their role in understanding the physical and emotional needs of their husbands. A joyful giving of one's self means more than living together until death do you part.

"Wives, love your husbands" is an exciting admonition. It is a married woman's life. She brings to marriage all her resources, all her potential, and under the tutelage of God she becomes what He wants her to be. For in the final analysis, His instructions are not so much obeyed by doing as by *being*.

DISCUSSION QUESTIONS

1. No word is misused in our society more than the word *love*. We say, "I love your hat," or "I love peanuts," or "I love you," or "I love God." We need to think about love's content. What definition or explanation of love in this essay was most meaningful to you? Do you have other thoughts to add which strengthen the concept of love?

2. Why is it true to say that any hope we have of loving others is found in God?

3. What are some goals a Christian wife should have for her husband? Husbands, what goals do you wish your wives had for you?

4. Why does it trouble some wives to have the husband declared "the head of the wife" (I Corinthians 11:3)? Look up the context of this verse and observe the relationship and responsibility the husband sustains. Does this change the picture in any way?

5. What problems come into a home when a wife does not obey the biblical instruction of Ephesians 5:22? What is to be the quality of her submission, according to this verse? According to Ephesians 5:24, may a wife choose the areas of submission she prefers?

6. This chapter states that "women are being molded by the times." What is the image of today's woman if one were to generalize on the American scene?

7. Suppose a woman wants her husband to be the leader in the home, but he is dragging his feet in taking his responsibility. What can a wife do to encourage him to take the role of leadership?

8. Today's mood is one of openness and honesty, of relatively easy recounting of personal life. What controls should be put on "telling it like it is" about one's personal relationships? Why is this so important?

9. Why are we sometimes so eager to criticize our marriage partners, but so slow to pray for them?

10. Wives, who are also mothers, often have so many demands on their time that they can begin to wonder who they are apart from their responsibilities. Every wife wants to be a person in her own right, not just John's wife or Sara's mother. How can wives order the priorities of life in such a way that they are living in biblical relationship to their families and themselves?

How to Be a Good Husband   **3**

WHENEVER THE WORDS *Be a Man!* are used to bolster up someone's flagging courage or his moral behavior, we understand the implications of these words. As C. S. Lewis observed, when one sees one crocodile eating another, he never says, "Be a crocodile!" We expect crocodiles to act that way. We have a manly standard for men. *Be a man* is a reminder that we are made in the image of God, capable of fellowship with God.

It's no mistake that the followers of Jesus Christ are called disciples. Being a disciple means being disciplined — disciplined in mind, body, and will. It's in line with *being a man.*

Being a good husband involves becoming what God had in mind when He made you a man. It's more than taking a wife and simply living with her. Being a good husband even goes beyond bringing home the bacon and giving the wife a generous household allowance. Cartoonists picture the tired husband coming home, handing his wife the paycheck, eating the food prepared for him, and reading the paper until he falls asleep in his chair. If that's all there is to living seven days a week, few wives would give that kind of a husband a passing grade.

Because God made a man to be more than this, He gave him special abilities, generally different from those women possess; and He expects man to use these abilities to express his manhood in the world. Generalizations are never a tight fit for every member of the race, but an attempt to define man's gifts and responsibilities help us to understand more of what is involved in being a man.

Objective reasoning is generally a masculine characteristic. While the woman may operate on the level of the emotions or intuition, a man often has a more logical approach and a cooler head in examining a problem. While the wife sees the details, the husband's view spans the big picture. Obviously these abilities vary, but they give man the insight to take the initiative in decision making.

Leadership is man's role in God's plan — leadership which affects the home and the church — and this requires taking initiative, making decisions, and the courage to do both. We like to think of the male role of courage in the face of physical danger, but even more important is courage in the area of moral decision. Man ought to be the leader and pacesetter in ethical conduct — and we ought to teach this to the boys growing up in our homes.

A man receives the authority for leadership in these areas from God. Happy is the wife who has a husband who doesn't shy away from the responsibilities of his manhood.

Yet if a man has a strong authoritative mother and has never seen his father exercise this kind of leadership, he may willingly abdicate both authority and responsibility in the home to his wife. He is relieved to have her run things. This leaves the wife without his support in household affairs. He retreats into his world, and life is soon without mutuality. Both husband and wife then suffer significant loss. Certainly wives get shortchanged in this kind of relationship.

GODLY MANHOOD

We've already agreed that being born *male* doesn't mean natural leadership. That's why God tells the wife to be submissive to the husband and not to compete for headship. But from the beginning God meant the man to be responsible (remember how He immediately set Adam to work by organizing creation and labeling its creatures?) and a leader, an initiator. For he was made in the image of God who offers help to any man who comes to Him. God gives His children an adequacy they can never have in themselves. Not every one will be alike in style of leadership, but God doesn't ask a man to lead his home and to make moral decisions without offering him any wisdom for the job.

Godly manhood, however, reflects the character of Jesus Christ. He never ran over others roughshod. He respected opinions; He was sympathetic to need; He blessed little children; He was tender and sensitive to those wounded by life; He made decisions; He knew where He was going; He led with conviction. A Christian man has God's sense of value of the worth of another person.

Godly leadership in the husband results from walking with God. A man leads his wife and his family, not by giving authoritative utterances, but by what he is. There must be content in his leadership. Empty, vain words and aggressive action do not prove either authority or wisdom. Authority for the sake of authority may just disclose an unreasonable, insecure father who has to dominate to bolster his own ego — and may produce a child who stammers, who has low self-esteem and a poor view of the Fatherhood of God — to say nothing of a browbeaten wife who feels inadequate or rebellious!

What we need are men who speak with *spiritual authority*. Don't confuse spiritual authority with being an authority on spiritual things. *Spiritual authority* reveals something about the inner life of the man. The character of God is worked into the character of the man. No man can have adequate direction for the total needs of others unless he is in regular conversation with God. A vigorous spiritual life will make use of all that is manly within him!

In such a context it is safe to talk about the husband as the authority in the home. As soon as the vows in the first marriage on earth were spoken, the Bible records the leadership of the man in Genesis 2:24: "Therefore a man leaves his father and mother and cleaves unto his wife, and they become one flesh." The man *leaves* and *cleaves*. He sets up a new home and he sets his mind to be faithful to the person and needs of his wife. And this encompasses so much, especially in light of all the facets of personhood.

HOW TO LOVE YOUR WIFE

While studying Ephesians 5 with a group of high school students, the question came up: Why does the Bible say for wives to submit and husbands to love? Don't wives need to love their husbands, too?

How would you answer that? Perhaps it is that God knows what instruction each needs most. When a wife submits, she *is* loving her husband, but all that is willful in her may resist doing this.

And it is easy for a husband, in the routine of life, to forget that his wife exists for more than meeting his needs. She may become a habit, rather than a person to be loved.

But the bigger, more overwhelming picture is this: In some mysterious way, a husband's relationship to his wife depicts Christ's relationship to the church. That's solemn business. Take a look at Ephesians 5:25-32. A husband is to love his wife as Christ loves the church — the same quality of love. That's a scary assignment.

How does Christ love the church? He gave Himself up for her. His love is *sacrificial*. But not without design. He is *purposeful* in His love. He has a high goal in mind for the church (v. 26), that He might sanctify her, that she might be holy and without blemish (v. 27). Certainly Christ is *realistic*. He knows who makes up the church, but He also sees what the church can become. His love is *constant, willful,* not dependent on His emotional feelings about the church. He *nourishes* it and *cherishes* it (v. 29). Why? Because we are members of His body. So, writes Paul, ought men to love their wives.

How much a husband needs his wife's help if he is to obey these instructions from God! How easy it is to submit to that kind of a husband! But notice that the instruction to both husbands and wives contain no "iffy" clauses — *if* he loves you this way, then submit, or *if* she submits, then love her as Christ loves the church.

WHAT MAKES A MARRIAGE CHRISTIAN?

The husband's obedience to God undergirds the very structure of marriage. He is responsible to God, not to his wife. The lines of authority are clear. The wife is responsible, in the Lord, to her husband.

This is God's standard, not man's. Obviously, if this is Christian marriage, two Christians marrying do not automatically have a Christian marriage. A Christian marriage is one which is formed and lived out under God's directive. Because it is so beautifully designed by Him, it results in oneness, with all the safety of relationship inherent in oneness.

Other instructions to husbands are found in I Peter 3 (along with some wisdom for wives). Peter says, "Live considerately with your wives, bestowing honor on the woman as the weaker sex, since you are joint heirs of the grace of life, in order that your prayers may not be hindred" (3:7).

Within this verse is enough practical wisdom to fill a counseling manual. Understanding and obeying this verse could make all the difference in marriage. It's a beautiful elaboration of what *loving* your wife really means. The dictionary defines *considerate*: being observant of the rights and feelings of others; showing thoughtfulness and kindness. *Thoughtfulness* is given as a synonym.

Being considerate doesn't mean that you'll do all your wife's work or become *her* helpmeet; but it might mean you'll sometimes offer practical assistance. It will always mean that you'll try to be sensitive to her need to be appreciated, to be understood, to have affection expressed. It means you'll have a high degree of empathy about what her life is like. It means you won't belittle her, take her for granted, or abuse her. It means you will act in honor regarding your rights to her person.

Why? Because you are heirs together of the grace of life. Because of Christ's death, you've received a joint inheritance. You share it together because you are one. That leaves no room for selfishly grabbing one's share of life's goodies — because God's kind of inheritance to husbands and wives is bound up in the oneness package.

The richness of the inheritance meets life's needs. It is *the grace of life*. Can you imagine life without *grace*, without that special God-like touch? Grace is bound up in the character of God who enriches us and doesn't deal with us according to our deservings. *The grace of life*. It's hard to define all that includes. It embodies all we can imagine of what the flavor of a Christian home should be with Christ's grace washing over its daily relationships.

The grace of life has come to us because Jesus Christ chose to grace this life with His presence. He is pleased to dwell with families today; He is willing to change homes, relationships, and attitudes. He is full of grace and truth; and when He is made the real head of the home, His character influences ours and produces, in both husband and wife, love, joy, peace, and all the other graces of life mentioned in Galatians 5:22.

We need to stir each other up to good works in living considerately together. Peter gives a convincing reason why: that your prayers won't be hindered. God doesn't promise to answer the prayers of the disobedient; but I sense even something further here. People who aren't living thoughtfully together probably don't pray together either. No closeness of spirit binds them to kneel humbly before the God who sees all of life.

A couple lived in seeming contentment for several years. Three children filled their home with delight. Life went along pleasantly; they were regular in attendance at church and faithful to each other. Then the oldest son became ill and his life seemed about to terminate. Both the husband and the wife lived in tension, often venting their emotions on the other. In their most desperate moment it occurred to them to pray. Weeping with relief before each other and God, they were bound together in newness of life in this near tragedy. It was the first time they had prayed aloud together about anything of deep feeling in their life together! Prayer had been offered at mealtime as a rote exercise.

The illness of that son became the biggest blessing of that marriage. Both husband and wife realized how little they really knew each other, how little they shared of real life — and how barren their life was before God.

Many couples seem embarrassed together in the presence of God. A husband, exercising his leadership, should put an end to that stalemate. Life has too many areas that need God's touch to keep silence before Him. And husbands and wives need to be bound together afresh by their appearance together at the throne of grace. Live considerately so that your prayers won't be hindered.

When husbands obey God, the home goes the right way and both husband and wife have optimum opportunity to experience the happiness and the contentment of a Christian home.

DISCUSSION QUESTIONS

1. What image comes to your mind when someone says, "Be a man!"? Which of these are valid in a biblical sense?

2. Discuss the necessity of teaching both men and boys the importance of responsibility in making moral decisions which affect ethical conduct. What might some of these moral decisions be?

Why should men be leaders in ethical conduct? How might a high view of his responsibility in this area affect a young man's dating conduct?

3. What kind of leadership do wives want?

4. What pressures in our society encourage men to abdicate their leadership in the home? What happens to the home when the husband does not assume his responsibility?

5. What is the difference between a man exercising authority and a man exercising spiritual authority? Define this carefully. Are there any areas of life in which authority should not be *spiritual?*

6. Whose responsibility is more difficult — the wife's to submit, or the husband's to love as Christ loved the church?

7. What makes a marriage Christian?

8. Discuss practical ways in which living considerately together would help the wife and the husband.

9. Dig into the richness of the phrase from I Peter 3:7, "joint heirs of the grace of life." What does this mean? How should the grace of life be exhibited in our homes? How would this affect our children, our guests, ourselves?

10. What practical suggestions can be made to help husbands and wives learn how to pray together?

4 Out of Silence into Dialog

SHARON WAS CLEARLY OUTRAGED. She burst in on my morning cup of coffee with the turbulence of a tornado. "I feel like a *thing*," she spouted off. "Is my conversation so unintelligent that I'm not worth talking to? He just doesn't say *anything* to me. I could be a post in the ground for all he bothers to communicate with me. All of a sudden I feel like I don't even know my own husband. It's as if he has been hiding from me for years!"

Usually so loyal and supportive of her husband, Sharon took me by surprise. She'd come to the end of her rope emotionally and had to sound off to someone. It was as if her humanity had been called into question by a husband who didn't bother to talk with her.

I remember thinking with amusement, *All over America in homes such as these this scene is taking place.* Only it wasn't funny. If you've ever lived in close relationship with someone who didn't bother to communicate, you know the frustration and loneliness of living with a silent Joe.

That's one side of the story. The other goes something like this. Pete, unaware that he has done something that offended Alice, feels the atmosphere freeze over. He may be slow to notice, but the icicles hanging in the air eventually become obvious. He inquires into the problem. Silence. He makes another stab at defining the tension. Icy silence, or a sharp retort. Unsure of how to stay the fury of a woman, he goes his own way and hopes for a thaw.

Obviously there are less traumatic levels of noncommunication within families. But lack of communication accumulates and bears seeds of discontent. Seething resentments erupt, triggered by an incident which under normal circumstances would seem quite unimportant. We can't get away with poor communication. We can't excuse ourselves by saying, "I find it difficult to communicate." God has made us word-partners with each other and with Himself. And while not all meaningful communication is verbal, some of it must be if we have the facility of speech.

Listening to each other is marvelous medicine in a marriage. Resentments need to be talked out, for they are the greatest danger to marital life. In 85 out of 100 couples visiting marriage counselors, the inability to communicate is a prime trouble factor. We don't come to marriage with well-developed communication techniques. In fact, two people marrying with a maximum of common factors in their background still are simply two different people. Think of your position in the family, your family life-style, your early experiences, your inherited characteristics ("You're just like your Aunt Jane!"), your educational exposure, your emotional makeup — think of all that has made you what you are! How can you expose all of this to the person with whom you are to become one? How can you be known?

Understanding each other takes time, but it also takes two people who are willing to share their inner selves. Marriage means the responsibility and privilege of being known by another person.

It may seem risky to be an open book; but when you agree to share the life of another person, you've already made the commitment to be known and to know, to be understood and to understand.

NONVERBAL COMMUNICATION

Nonverbal communication — the understanding look, a touch of the hand, special expressions of appreciation or affection — are sometimes more appropriate than many words. Or more plainly, a conversation may be the wrong approach at times. When a husband comes home irritated by a dozen frustrations too tiresome to recount to his wife, it helps if she shows she understands by her tenderness, by the way she manages family life or the children's conversation at the dinner table. By so doing she communicates psychological support and loving acceptance which speaks louder than words. If the details are important, she has made the way open for him to tell her about it later. The husband who has this same sensitivity to his wife's needs can offer healing balm to her tensions in similar ways.

A wise husband keeps the calendar in mind and offers special psychological support if his wife becomes curiously irrational or emotional for seemingly no good reason. The monthly cycle affects each woman differently, but for many it is a time of intense emotional stress. A wife ought not to have to raise a flag to announce her chemical changes more than once or twice if the husband is at all alert. His perceptive, understanding love will buoy up a wife's spirits and will help him avoid open confrontations during this time. If insurance companies find this a factor in accidents which involve women, and if large firms curtail the purchases of women buyers for three days during a month, then the emotional economics of the home ought to operate with similar care.

But these are only two examples of the times when a squeeze of the hand or a tender look communicate concern, understanding and love. Life's emergencies often call for positive nonverbal communication.

Negative nonverbal communication is another matter! It's the opposite of the tender look; it's the look that destroys. It's the shrug of the shoulder that says, "I could care less," or "How could you be such a stupid, callous oaf!" It's a neat way to cut someone down, but it's downright cowardly. If you have a complaint, at least have the courage to discuss it openly so that understanding and love can build and heal. Unspoken disapproval or detachment is devastating to a marriage.

OUR ALONENESS

Everyone knows loneliness. The most gregarious person you know has times of intense aloneness when there seems to be no one who understands, no one who can reach inside to the real person. Often in the middle of a large crowd, we feel most lonely. Loneliness creates a painful yearning to share one's self in some depth with another who really understands. We feel an incompleteness without a close relationship to another.

Ideally marriage is at least a partial solution to a person's loneliness. But, as Ruell Howe comments, there can be no relationship without dialog. Marriage can be shared loneliness between two strangers who live in the same house. Dispelling loneliness requires two people set free from the natural tendency to hide, to carry on one's own life independently of another. It requires a commitment to the other person's needs.

The fact of man's loneliness has theological implications. Each person is an individual, living within his own body, alone. In that sense, he is always lonely. And that restless, lonely feeling is part of God's design. The empty spot within is a God-shaped hole, and only He can really fill it. Man's aloneness is relieved only when God becomes the center of his life. Dwight Small has commented that loneliness is the voice of God calling us back to our lives as they were meant to be. Human love can never take the place of God, and if we are to be free to share our inner selves with any sense of identity or integrity, our spirit must find its rest in God. It is He who said, "I am with you always."

THE DESIRE TO COMMUNICATE

Communication is a matter of the spirit. It is one person reaching out to another, willingly giving up aloneness in order to be known. It does not need to be verbal, but it must touch the spirit of another so that both feel a sense of closeness.

Sometimes people settle for a very superficial kind of conversation that glosses over the top of life, and they mistake this for communication. A man may handle problems all day and feel he has done his share of communicating before he ever arrives home. Or perhaps he works on a machine and gets used to living within his own soul, and becomes less and less verbal. If there are children, marriage conversation can be a jumble of questions, a discussion of the day's simplicities and domestic crises. Unless a couple really desires a breakthrough to each other, they may never get below the surface. They will find it increasingly difficult to talk on the level of feelings, fears, hopes, and needs.

Life is increasingly distracting. Men drive further to work; wives are more involved outside the home; children have more activities. Communication demands a high degree of *want to,* a high sense of personal commitment. Communication is always getting outside of yourself to the other person, and our natural bent is to live inside ourselves.

Communicating means mutual self-disclosure. That's why a wife who talks and shares and reveals her deepest feelings doesn't feel like she has really communicated unless there is some response. Communication is self-disclosure, but it is also letting another person get inside of you with his self-disclosure. It's a two-way process.

Revealing one's self demands honesty. A phony kind of role playing destroys the heart of communication because it is a lie. Real intimacy is a costly involvement, not a forced-growth plant. It involves a level of trust, of the possibility of hurt or being misunderstood. Still there is no room for wearing masks. The heart of communication is openness and honesty.

Women generally are better at self-disclosure than men. Sometimes they are too good at it, and talk without listening or waiting for an answer. They interrupt the man once he does begin to unwind, and never realize they have taken back the ball and the game has only one participant.

THE RESPONSIBILITY TO COMMUNICATE

But that doesn't let men off the hook. That's what communication is all about. That's what honesty is for. Communication within marriage should make both people more sensitive and thoughtful. Better to say, "Will you please be quiet and *hear* what I'm saying?" than to beat a retreat and hide. It takes two to have a dialog.

The dignity of personhood demands that each partner be taken seriously and be known. Communication is love's commitment to see that this happens. Men or women who don't talk easily make a commitment to do so as the needs of the relationship require. Some get by with less real dialog than others. Much talking does not necessarily mean communication. But we have a *responsibility* to communicate.

Sometimes after a misunderstanding, instead of discussing the issues openly with apologies, a man will try to communicate through sexual advances that he is willing to forget. If that satisfies the wife, then that's agreeable. But if her need is to talk, and sex becomes a substitute for the courage of conversation, then the man is failing in his responsibility.

In reverse, a wife sometimes makes her point of disapproval by punishing her husband by refusing to give herself. A miserable buildup of resentments can accumulate unless genuine dialog takes place.

Happy indeed is the couple who clear the decks and agree beforehand that they will talk things out rather than fill emotional closets with ragged relationships. One of the family members must insist on meaningful communication. Blessed are the peacemakers who take the initiative in healing tensions.

Not long ago my husband said to me, as we were riding along in the car, "Fifteen minutes ago our silence was comfortable and supportive. All of a sudden it's not. I can feel it. What happened?"

He was right. I was reacting to a comment he

had made, and while I was not aware of the change in the quality of silence, he was. Sometimes silence is beautiful and comforting. Other times it strains for understanding and action.

THE JOY OF KNOWING EACH OTHER

I like holding hands mentally with my husband across the room. We know the other's reaction because we've lived together and exposed ourselves to each other on the level of ideas and feelings. We're finding the more this goes on, the more meaningful our nonverbal communication is. Our hearts talk the same language. It's the delicious state of feeling safe and loved and known.

Love expressed in genuine communication frees a person to be who he really is. There's a liberty, an individuality that expresses itself in personal life while at the same time uniting two people in closer bonds of oneness. Individual fulfillment heightened; oneness strengthened — this is the liberty of those who communicate.

But loving each other this way demands that we love God first and foremost. We love because He first loved us. When a couple live out Christ's love, they are on solid loving ground. They communicate from their deepest selves because the washing of Christ's love and forgiveness has freed them to do so. They can forgive one another because they know the cleanness of personal forgiveness. They can build into each other's lives because Christ has first built into their own.

Forgiveness must be a daily habit. This must be genuine forgiveness, not a condescending kind of pity that retracts its benefits if the person doesn't measure up. If we have any sense of our own sinfulness in God's eyes, if we have known forgiveness, we *must* be forgiving in personal relationships. Nothing stymies marital bliss more than collecting another's sins. James 5:16 tells us to confess our faults to each other and pray for each other. One thing we should know for certain about ourselves: we are sinners. We are quick to agree that our mates are also sinners. It should not surprise us that sinners *sin*. While we must encourage each other to holiness, we hardly do this by pretending not to sin. Realizing our common sinnerhood, there is plenty of room in life for daily forgiveness. "I'm sorry, dear," are important words in a marriage.

Sharing life on a spiritual plane brings new dimensions of communication, a focal point for life together. When channels are open to God, they are open to one another. If God's kind of love is flowing through a person, he cannot remain closed off from his mate. Praying together in His presence is the sweetest kind of sharing.

We *can* communicate because God took the initiative in communicating to us in Christ Jesus. And the Great Communicator has offered His help in the person of the Holy Spirit. Have you asked for His help lately?

DISCUSSION QUESTIONS

1. In what ways does communication affect our view of ourselves?

2. What ground rules would encourage better communication within a marriage? What levels of communication do you feel necessary in your marriage?

3. What is the value of verbal or nonverbal communication in your own personal needs? Dis-

cuss the destructive ways in which negative non-verbal communication operates.

4. Discuss the significance of the statement that *without dialog there is no relationship.*

5. How is man's problem of aloneness most fully resolved? Is this true to your own experience? Can you give a specific example?

6. In what ways can we deceive ourselves into thinking we are communicating when we are not?

7. Why are women generally better at self-disclosure than men?

8. What is the key to opening up communication channels?

9. Theodore Bovet, commenting on the need for continual forgiveness within marriage says, "We must be Christs to one another." Why is forgiveness so important in marriage? What is to be the quality of this forgiveness? See Ephesians 4:32.

10. Try this experiment in your discussion. Give each person five slips of paper. Without taking much time, ask each person to write on each slip a word which describes the kind of person he is. Then ask him to place these slips in order of importance.

Dependent on time and the constituency of the group, divide the group into smaller sections and have each person share his list. If the group is composed entirely of couples, perhaps the most worthwhile sharing would be in husband-wife breakdowns.

5 Discipline Makes Disciples

DISCIPLINE PRODUCES DISCIPLES. The words come from the Latin *discipulus*, to learn. Discipline is training which corrects, molds, strengthens or perfects. It implies an authority, a standard. It is a positive concept, not a negative one.

That takes the hickory stick out of discipline. Mention *discipline* and some immediately think of sitting on a stool facing the corner. To them discipline equals punishment. Discipline *may* involve a hickory stick, but not just for the sake of punishment. It is everything you do in order to help a person learn to be what he ought to be.

Discipline is a basic building block for life, and the contrast between a disciplined and an undisciplined person bears this out. I think of Jerry who wanted to give his life to God. He professed faith in Christ and began making feeble efforts to get to know Him. But Jerry had no discipline in his life. He had never been trained to order his habits in any way or to do what was right regardless of its convenience. He had little self-control and stumbled into sin without resistance. He had grown up without discipline; he was undisciplined in school; he did not succeed in his first year at college. He had small resources to help him be a disciple of Jesus Christ.

Discipline, therefore, is not a children's word; it

is a life word. Undisciplined people live careless lives which bring distress to others. Grown-ups who aren't disciplined have trouble being disciples of Jesus Christ; they lack consistent work patterns; they make poor use of their gifts of time and energy.

Discipline is different from rigidity. The inflexibility of a kind of Prussian authoritarianism is a poor brand of discipline. Discipline should correct, not foster rebellion. Being disciplined implies a built-in ability to do what is right. Discipline has a long range goal: maturity.

John, father of six in our town, barks out orders to his children like a tough top sergeant. They line up and obey, but the "discipline" he claims to have appears to be for John's convenience rather than for the strengthening of a child's ability to do right. The children are more robots than people with needs. Their response satisfies some unrealistic ego need John has. If he continues to be unreasonable as the children grow older, he will provoke them to wrath.

Discipline does not make rules more important than people. It is because people are so *very* important that there must be discipline. Discipline and love are related.

SELF-DISCIPLINE

Sally says she is a Type B. She functions poorly in the morning and well late at night. She conceded to being this kind of person without much struggle. So for most of the fifteen years of her married life she slept in while her husband and children got themselves off to work and school. She told the story openly as if it was a big joke, but I think on the inside she knew it was not.

Sally had settled for some inferior goals. She had only short range value: two or three hours of extra sleep. The value she had not weighed was that of a mother's influence in setting the tone for the day and seeing that the people she loved began the day with good food, proper clothing, and prayer before leaving the house. Sally always said her children didn't eat much breakfast anyway, and they were happy in this pattern.

But her children had nothing else to compare it with. When Sally finally disciplined herself to be a responsible wife and mother, she began seeing some of the "peaceable fruit" of discipline in the lives of her children. She found they *did* eat breakfast when she prepared it. The day began in a more orderly way for everyone. Praying at the beginning of the day did something for the whole family.

From beginning to end in household affairs when people aren't disciplined to do what is right, life limps along less effectively and happily. Freedom multiplies in the disciplined household.

The same thing is true in a person's life with God. No one has extra hours lying around for personal Bible reading. Anyone who spends time with God in prayer and Bible reading does so because he disciplines himself. He does it because it is good and right, and the result is growth and maturity.

Mothers and fathers must discipline themselves if they would be disciples. It is no good teaching the commandments of God without personal obedience. Disciplined parents are the ones who will be effective in disciplining their children. They will do it according to principle, not passion.

GOD'S DISCIPLINE

Human beings have two basic needs: discipline and love. Discipline without love is tyranny. Love without discipline is sentiment. The goal of discipline is always maturity. This is why God disciplines us. He gives us a pattern for personal discipline and for disciplining our children in the way He cares for us.

Hebrews 12:5-11 discusses God's discipline. The King James version uses the word *chastens* and *chastisement,* which is defined as *punishment* in contemporary English. *Discipline* is a better translation; however, punishment is inevitably part of correcting our wayward tendencies. We are told not to lose courage when we are punished by God, nor to regard His discipline lightly. For,

(1) Discipline gives security. God cares enough about us to train us so that our behavior becomes what it should be. It is a proof that He loves us.

(2) Discipline is for our good. At the time it seems painful rather than pleasant (v. 10) but God has in mind that we should share His holiness.

(3) Discipline yields the fruits of righteousness to those who are trained by it (v. 11). Discipline is training for righteous living. God has a high goal in mind for His children. He is not afraid to use discipline to see the goal accomplished.

PARENTAL DISCIPLINE

Parental discipline helps transfer the fruit of God's discipline into the lives of our children. Parents are God's chosen agents, and in a sense stand in God's place until the child is older. Parents are *not* God; however they are responsible to Him. A parent can say to a child, "Learn to obey me

47

now, so you will know how to obey God later." Wise discipline provides a secure environment in which to grow up. Someone cares. Someone knows what the standard is.

Child psychologists believe that discipline is necessary for mental health. It makes us feel terribly insecure not to know where the fences which surround our lives are located. It's frightening because it may mean no one knows. Where may you run? How far may you go? Teen-agers have made open pleas in youth panels and in letters to newspaper advice columns asking for ground rules, because they know that these mean "someone cares about me."

The Book of Proverbs contains abundant instructions on raising children. Proverbs 19:18 says, "Discipline your son while there is hope; do not set your heart on his destruction."

Proverbs 29:17 reads, "Discipline your son, and he will give you rest; he will give delight to your heart."

Proverbs 22:6 tells us to "Train up a child in the way he should go, and when he is old he will not depart from it."

Train a child while he is young. Take into consideration his whole person. Do not let him go his own way, yet at the same time give him an adequate view of self. Our goal is not to break the child's spirit but to channel it. Punishment for disobedience is a fact in God's economy. Our children should learn that we uphold this standard. But discipline is far more creative, less one-sided than this. It is building into the life some concept of self-esteem, the ability to choose wisely and a respect for the authority of God.

Wise discipline requires special help from God. Some children are crushed by strong words; others respond only to a spanking. A spanking doesn't phase others; they need to be denied choice privileges. We need always to remember that children are people, that love and discipline go together, and that our goal is maturity.

We discipline because it is right to do so, because we are concerned about righteousness. While anger is not an adequate motive for discipline, I am inclined to think that it is not always wrong to be aroused to anger over our children's disobedience.

Recently I heard a father tell of his son's repeated lack of response to his mother's call to come upstairs. Five, six times — still no response. The father finally stopped his gentle urgings that his son obey and spanked the boy all the way up the stairs to the mother. Sensitive to his anger, the father later apologized to the boy. I am quite sure the father was more sensitive than the boy. The son had a sense of justice; he knew he deserved it. The father would have done well to have acted sooner. There will be times when we need to apologize for our behavior to our children — and we must do this. But anger at their behavior which brings about just discipline is not necessarily one of those times.

GROUND RULES FOR DISCIPLINE

Here are some ground rules for disciplining children:

(1) Keep your word. Make no idle threats or promises. Be careful that you don't make unimportant negatives for the child to lash out against, which will force you to back down on your word. Don't make promises you don't expect to keep.

Then insist that their word be kept as carefully as yours.

(2) Don't harangue. It's hard to find the off-switch on some mothers once they get started scolding. Bringing up every past wrong in the course of the scolding defeats the child and leaves the feeling that nothing is ever forgotten. Speak carefully and mean what you say.

My nephew once remarked, "My mother gets her point across to us just by giving us the old hairy eyeball!" Which was his way of saying, "We know her standards, and all it takes is a look from her."

(3) Don't argue. Have a discussion, perhaps, as the child grows older. But if you give in to arguing, whining, and crying, you'll have plenty of it to cope with. Parents generally get from their children what they ask for. Some parents put up with a great deal of needless inconvenience, which is of no benefit to the child, because they insist on too little. Children understand more than we think!

(4) Be just. Children have an acute sense of fair play. If punishment is involved, make it fit the situation. You are teaching what is morally and socially important. If you treat careless milk-spilling in the same way you treat telling a lie, you make milk-spilling and lie-telling of the same moral importance. And they are not!

(5) Teach your child the importance of a genuine admission of guilt. "I'm sorry" are perhaps the hardest words in the English language to say but these words are most easily learned when the child is small. Don't ever accept glibness in their usage, however.

I remember taking our three-year-old to the

neighbor's house with the firm instruction that he was to address her by name, look at her face while he spoke, and tell her he was sorry for picking her prize tulips. It never occurred to him or to me that he wouldn't do exactly what I had said he should. It was very important to me to train him to look someone in the eye and say, "I'm sorry." How cowardly are the foot-shufflers, who look the other way, while they mumble out an apology with the sincerity of a fish!

(6) Teach your child that forgiveness is real. Let him know you face common sinnerhood together, but teach him by your example that you know what forgiveness is all about.

(7) Discuss situations which reflect on life's values whenever you can as the child grows older, so that he can construct his own value structure. Let him help make decisions. The goal is maturity. On unimportant matters, be prepared to let him make a few mistakes as a learning process. Make it easy for him to admit poor judgment and give him confidence to try again.

(8) Go to God regularly for help and wisdom. Then act confidently, with a strong note of certainty. He who hesitates finds reluctant obedience. Pray daily that your children's hearts will be available to the promptings of the Holy Spirit.

We discipline our children because it is the loving thing to do. God has a high standard for them, and we uphold this standard. We are agents in building character, in curbing the traits that would lead to folly. We discipline our children so they can learn to discipline their own lives. We do this more effectively if they can see that we, also, have learned this. Our goal is maturity and self-control. We want them to know what is valuable.

Discipline opens up a life of freedom to those trained by it. Real freedom is freedom to choose what is right. The undisciplined person is pushed about by life. He often is a slave to himself, to his own lack of self-control.

Discipline yields peaceable fruits of righteousness in our lives and in the lives of our children. It is the password to freedom; it gives delight to the heart.

DISCUSSION QUESTIONS

1. Define discipline carefully.

2. What are the evidences of lack of discipline in a person's life? In a household?

3. What is the difference between discipline and rigidity? How does each affect an individual's personality?

4. How does discipline affect one's spiritual life?

5. What does God's discipline in our lives do for us?

6. What are the peaceable fruits of righteousness? How does the exercise of discipline produce these?

7. What are the basic needs of every human being? Why are these important to us?

8. Describe the tone of family life brought about by using the ground rules of discipline. What would be present in the home? What absent? Do you have additional ground rules which add to the true concept of discipline?

9. Why is it important that you discipline with confidence? What action should you take if you find you have disciplined wrongly?

10. Discuss how freedom and discipline are related in personal life.

Living Together As a Christian Family 6

JANET AND I WERE SITTING in the university student union making a pretense at drinking the strong bitter coffee which must have come from the bottom of the pot. She had asked if we could meet to talk, and I found her direct, intelligent, eager to communicate how she felt inside. I wanted to listen and understand what was happening in her life with God. She spoke with intense feeling, and what she said teaches us something about the Christian home.

"When I was home I just fit into the pattern, never questioning what I had been taught. I believed all about God and Christ and the Bible. But since I've been here I've tried to evaluate what the essence of Christian faith is as I've experienced it. Frankly, when I look back on my home and my church I don't think of a loving group of people, full of concern for each other. I don't think of reality in knowing God. I just think of people going through the ritual, all wearing masks.

"It has come to me with alarming clarity that the Christians I know not only don't *love* each other, they don't even *know* each other. Nobody in our family ever talked about how they *felt in-*

This chapter first appeared in *The Church Herald* of May 2, 1969, and is used with permission.

side about anything. We went to church and talked about God and truth, but I knew enough of what was going on in some families to know that there were brokenhearted people, disappointed with life, lonely people in those pews. But nobody ever talked about that level of life.

"Within our own family I knew my mother didn't tell my father how lonely she often felt, how she didn't feel needed, how she wished he would talk to her. She just kept busy with committees, pretending these other things didn't matter. Yet I know she hurt inside about this. But we never talked or prayed about how we felt inside — nothing was ever on the level of the real *you*. We were always acting out some kind of unreal, victorious superexistence.

"I've watched this — this phony kind of role playing — and I've about come to the conclusion that if this is what it means to be a Christian, if this is Truth — then you may be right, but I don't think I'm interested. I want warmth and openness and honesty in my relationships."

I had heard it all before, sometimes with different details, but the heart of the issue is the same. This generation wants honesty in relationships as never before! Perhaps it's the impersonal world in which we live, where people are numbers, IBM cards, often nameless and faceless. Maybe it is a sharpened perception about the world. The young are exposed to a wider, rawer world than their parents ever knew. Seeing it "like it is" disillusions people and makes them hungry for honesty, suspicious of people who have told them half-truths and won't admit to the other half.

When I listen to collegians spell out their disillusionment, I want to paint huge signs and put them on the front lawn of every church: WANTED:

THOROUGHLY CHRISTIAN HOMES. We don't need better church programs, additional youth pastors, more catechism, more conferences on youth needs. We need better Christian homes.

ACCEPTANCE WITHIN THE FAMILY

What should characterize a Christian home? What should it offer its members? Acceptance. The kind of acceptance that allows you to be the *real* you. It includes love, which always desires the other's highest good but which can be misunderstood, a smothering concept in some people's minds. Acceptance means you are valuable in that home just because you are *you*. It reflects God's kind of love.

It means that the child who likes folk-rock has a hearing, an acceptance equal to the child who likes Bach and sings only hymns. It means you talk about how a person feels inside, about what he likes, and why he feels that way. Father doesn't snort off his prejudice without listening or ignore you because he doesn't care.

A Christian home is a safe place to try out your ideas, to verbalize what you believe is valuable, without being shot down. You are taken seriously. Here you can express even your heretical thoughts. Instead of being told that nice people don't think that way, there is an opportunity for intelligent discussion and questioning. Thoughtful leadership is given in discovering what is true and valuable and good. A Christian home is a safe place: not safe in the sense that you are never corrected, never made to make amends for wrong-doing — but safe in the sense that your person is taken seriously. You get the idea that you are valuable there.

I have seen more conflict in families over the length of a boy's hair than almost any other single behavior item. Father doesn't think any decent, respectable boy would wear his hair like that; and besides, what will others think if he lets his boy look like that? The son, on the other hand, looks at his great grandfather's picture hanging in the hall and wonders when the length of hair became a moral issue. All communication stops — on every subject. Hair has clouded even the ability to discuss openly the reality of trusting Jesus Christ. An amoral thing — the length of hair — creates a chasm neither father nor son can leap across.

Hair length is only one example. It could be a disagreement on any contemporary fad or personal habit which flares up between family members, paralyzing and fencing off individuals who need to talk together about the real things of life. Like a red flag in a bullring, the response can be so irrational that we no longer hear what the other person is trying to say. We give up intelligent reasoning to the pressure of emotional tension.

That's a travesty on a Christian home. If Jesus Christ is the center of the home, the source of all reality, that makes the home Christian. Somehow I can't imagine Him and His pervading presence letting us get so sidetracked. He said Himself that men who judge only from the outward appearance judge amiss. I can't believe that He, whose knowledge spans the cultures of all time, always agrees with our value structure. It often needs evaluation. He may not care about the length of hair. He *does* care about rebellion in the heart. He cares about the inner person, not the exterior trimmings. If our home adequately represents Jesus Christ, if He controls our family conduct, then we get across the idea that He looks at the heart, that He cares about honesty and about principles. By our emphasis we show what we think is morally important and what the unchanging principles really are.

HONESTY AND LOVE

Jesus Christ unites families who pray together; not droning prayers which are so much alike that the children can guess what words come next, but prayers about the real stuff of life — loss of temper, poor attitudes, laziness, thoughtlessness, an understanding heart, rapport with a teacher — anything that touches that day and the people in it. He honors parents who confess, in the presence of children who already know it, that they are sinners. He blesses children who can say they are sorry and show spontaneous love. He forgives people. He heals the wounds and restores family joy.

Jesus Christ loves sinners, not sin. We ought to be like Him in our homes, distinguishing one from the other. Pretending, covering up sin, has kept people living as strangers in the same house. What strange unchristian pride keeps us from putting our finger on the wrong and saying, "I'm sorry," or, "I need help"? What silly self-consciousness keeps us from expressing love — not a cloying, sentimental kind of envelopment that suffocates a person — but the wholesome kind of expression that frees a person to be his best?

Love ought to flow out of the doors of our homes because we are daily experiencing authentic Christian fellowship within our families — fellowship which includes honesty, self-exposure, and forgiveness because home is such a safe place.

I don't know what it was like to see a Christian home in the first century, but I suspect such a home shone like a bright light. I can imagine the Roman world commenting on the husband's love for the wife, the wife's attitude toward her husband and children, the open fellowship of the family, their communication with God, a God so real He invaded every part of their lives.

Contemporary homes ought to be beacons of such reality. I'm not talking about the neighbors observing that we go to church and don't wash our car on Sunday. I mean that Jesus Christ would be so real in family life that no one would have to hide, to pretend, to wear a mask. Daily forgiveness would be a genuine experience. Interfamily communication would be the hallmark of our family life because we are so honest and open before each other and the Lord. Having His perspective, we would major on major themes, and put minor ones in their place of importance. And above all, our love for Jesus Christ would be more conspicuous than our religious observances.

We read in the Acts of the Apostles how unbelievers were attracted to Jesus Christ and joined in the fellowship and sharing of God's Word within the early Christian homes. That's how they got their name. Others referred to them as the Christones, Christians. Our homes, by displaying this quality in our family fellowship, this integrity in our lives, and this outreach in our love, must be this same kind of witness.

WHERE TO BEGIN

Nice, you say. But how do you go about having that kind of Christian home?

The key is *your* life with God. If your relationship with Jesus Christ is vital, your family will know it. They will know it, not by your pontifical utterances, but by your love, your willingness to listen to an idea different from your own, your patience, your personal honesty, your obedience. It's contagious when it is authentic. If you're a parent, it should begin with you and God. If you're a child, it *could* begin with you.

One of the most creative exercises in the world is taking the Word of God and letting its truth cut into your personal life. Our children ought to observe the Scriptures changing us. They need to talk with us about the practical, piercing application of its message to daily life. Do your children believe that the Bible is an alive, relevant, life-changing book, or have they classified it with the dull, religious volumes of the past? We ought to get quite excited about the fact that we have a message from God!

A second creative exercise is remembering that children are people from the minute they are born. Some people make the mistake of admitting children into full-fledged *peoplehood* only after they are out of school. People need to begin speaking about what is inside when they are little so they can continue communicating as they grow up — so they get used to having their thinking listened to, challenged, and believed. Talk together about the day, about God, about disappointments, about love.

There is a wise saying: Give your children experiences, not things. Experiences mean doing things together, sharing intimate moments that bind you together. It sometimes means putting these moments into words to increase their meaningfulness. A world of creative thinking and doing is involved here. It involves God and His world and you and all the little people God puts in your home. It means knowing Him together and being so glad about it that communication is just the natural overflow of hearts filled with His love. Then the world looks on and says, "*That* is a Christian home."

DISCUSSION QUESTIONS

1. What does Janet's conversation point out about interfamily communication? In what ways do you identify with her comments?

2. What are the hindrances to genuine communication on the family level?

3. How would you define what the feeling of acceptance within the family does for a person? In what ways does this develop personality?

4. How are acceptance and love related? What happens to the child when acceptance or love is communicated to him on the basis of his performance?

5. What does God's example in loving us teach us about acceptance of others?

6. Why is it important to discuss the *feeling-level* of life within the family? What keeps us from doing this?

7. Suppose you are a member of a family which seldom communicates on the level of how people really feel inside. What can you do to break through communication barriers?

8. In what ways can parental standards for children be selfish? How does this relate to admitting children to full fledged *peoplehood* as mentioned in this chapter?

9. Who must change if communication is to take place when there is tension — the parent or the child?

10. This chapter says the key to breakthrough in interfamily communication is your life with God. What potential change does this offer family life?

Family Adventures
with God

7

A VERY WISE AND LOVING KING called a simple subject of his kingdom into his inner chamber. The man was neither rich nor knowledgeable, and was very humble in the presence of the king, feeling his great unworthiness. The king, seeing his fear, invited him to eat at his table. It was food such as the man had never seen before and it satisfied him as none before ever had.

When he had finished eating, the king explained the great honor he was about to give the man. The king asked the simple servant to be his steward and be responsible for a treasure box he would give him. In the treasure box, said the king, were words — only they were not ordinary words. They were like choicest meat and finest drink. Whoever ate these words and assimilated them into his person found he did not feel hungry or thirsty anymore. Besides this, his eyesight became so improved that he saw things in life he had never seen before. What had once seemed of great value was seen for its real worth, and what had seemed of lesser importance now became very valuable. Indeed, those who would eat would find themselves partaking of the king's wisdom.

The simple servant, who was now a steward, was awed with his responsibility. He carefully opened the cover of the box and read, "Whoever eats these words eats the words of life." He recognized the value of the treasure and asked how he might keep it safely. But the king said, "Share my treasure throughout the realm. Eat generously of it yourself and give it to your wife and children without measure. It shall be life to your soul and marrow to your bones. The supply shall not diminish with much eating."

What did the man do with the treasure chest? Some say that as time went by he put the chest on the shelf of his house where his wife carefully dusted it each week. He ate only sparingly and fed his children likewise. His strength was irregular and he often hungered for worthless food and his eyesight grew poor. He saw his children stumble on the path and he forgot that within the chest was the way of life.

End of story. You can make up a better ending if you like. In fact, I hope it is not your story. For what could be greater folly than possessing a great supply and failing to eat the words of life, words which give perspective and light on the way! Yet within the English-speaking world are more translations of the Scripture in contemporary language than is known anywhere else. The treasures of God's Word are so readily available. But many who have eaten at the King's table have become poor stewards of the treasure and wonder that their lives are under greater stress and their hearts are less light and their children less godly.

I think of the Congolese boy who had received his first copy of the Bible in his language and said, "This book makes holes in my heart. It understands me." I hear of Christians in Russia who write down the words of Scripture as they are dictated over shortwave missionary radio stations, so hungry are they to possess the treasure. Illiterate tribal people who have only short portions of the Bible translated into their language gather around the literate one of the village to hear the words of God. And I marvel at our values, our priorities and our lethargy.

PERSONAL LIFE WITH GOD

The most fruitful Bible reading comes out of personal hunger for God. Feeding ourselves spiritual food always requires discipline because we are going against the trend of the natural. We begin disciplining ourselves when we see how much we need to have God's thought patterns worked into our own. It *does* make a difference in daily life. Out of his heart a man speaks — and thinks and acts and is!

We each need God's Word to cut into our lives with the edge of truth. We need its guidance, its correction, its discipline. Our children need to see God's Word changing us. Biblical principles should be the framework from which we operate our homes. Most of the difficulties in personal life hark back to inadequate knowledge of biblical principles and a poor view of God.

We study the Bible, not so much to get a verse to bless us or a spiritual kick that we can share emotively with others, but to see God's principles at work in the world. Knowing about Daniel and the lion's den is different from understanding the principles of God's dealings with men. When we see the latter, the incidents of biblical history have new meaning.

I believe one of the reasons God has so carefully recorded the history of Israel for us is that Israel's story is the history of mankind in a microcosm. It is God reaching out to man to communicate Himself, His way, His truth. All of the story of mankind is condensed for us in Israel's history.

We read a review of this in Psalm 78 — a recitation of the faithfulness of God, of His intervention to deliver man and a recitation of the waywardness of man. Read the Psalm and compile the lists of the deeds of God and the wanderings of man.

All of the social issues and the tragedies of life are the result of mankind's endeavor to run his own life. Every famine victim, every hippie on LSD, every mother wondering if her child will return home safely from school, every illicit sex act, every family quarrel, every widow worrying behind locked doors and windows — can trace the problem he is facing back to man's waywardness. It is the accumulated result of our trying to run our lives, our homes, our cities, our nations without God. Israel's history is not a series of remote truths. It is the inescapable evidence of cause and effect.

More sobering is the fact that Israel's history is *my* history; it is *your* history. We have ample evidence of God — His saving power, His steadfast love, His provision, His forgiveness. Yet we often turn aside and forget Him. We run our own lives as if He did not exist, as if we could handle things without Him. We seek what we need elsewhere.

God says to us, I want to feed you with the finest of wheat, and satisfy you with honey from the Rock (Psalm 81:16) — but we turn elsewhere for food and drink. We may not mean to do this, but we show by our attitude towards God's Word what our choices are.

My people, says God, in Jeremiah 2:13, have committed two evils: they have forsaken me, the fountain of living waters, and hewed out cisterns for themselves, broken cisterns, that can hold no water. We can be the people of God, but live in a waste place because of our choices. Every time we take the Word of God lightly, mouth over its truths with no intent to obey, and run our own lives without the governing principle of God's Word — we are forsaking Him for other fountains. We demonstrate what we believe is valuable.

The miracle of it all is that God continually seeks the fellowship of believers. Jesus Christ said in John 14:23, "If a man loves me, he will keep my word and my Father will love him, and we will come to him and make our home with him." What a gracious offer! If we seek Him and love Him, He comes to us and reveals Himself to us (14:21).

No one else can live *your* spiritual life with God. Christianity is a very personal matter. Your openness to God's Word and your prayer life will define your life's pattern. Time spent with God is profitable because His Word 1) cleanses us; 2) renews our purpose; 3) changes our attitudes; and 4) gives us God's point of view about ourselves, Himself and the world.

SHARING GOD'S LIFE TOGETHER

As God's servants we are responsible for the Word of God. Paul speaks about being "intrusted with the gospel" (I Thess. 2:4). He also says in Romans 3:2 that the advantage of being a Jew is that to them was entrusted the oracles of God. We might pose a different question: Is there an advantage to being born in a Christian family? Yes, because the Word of God is entrusted to that family.

We pick up this same idea in Psalm 78 where the psalmist writes that God gave a testimony to Jacob and appointed His law in Israel, and commanded our fathers to teach it to their children (v. 5). Why was this so important? So that the next generation might know God's law, and that children yet unborn might be able to tell their children (v. 6). The end result is that they *should set their hope in God and not forget the works of God* (v. 7). Christian parents are (1) responsible to God for the Word of God and (2) responsible to teach it to their children.

My grandfather was a Dutch immigrant with ten children, and he took seriously his responsibility for the Word of God in the lives of his children. It was family custom that the Scripture be read at the close of every meal for which the family gathered. He didn't check out the psychological effect of this on his children; it never occurred to him to stop the practice because the children wiggled. He did it because it was right and he was responsible. Because he obeyed, my father learned to be a faithful Christian father to us and carried out the same pattern. In our home no one thought of leaving the table after any meal until we had read the Scripture. We had food to nourish us physically; then we had food to nourish us spiritually. It was built into life as part of our daily nourishment, like a spiritual dessert.

Recently, in recounting this to a group of Christian parents, one of the fathers asked me if we didn't all grow up being very resentful against our parents and Christianity. I'm always surprised when someone gives this reaction, because exactly the opposite is true. Proof of this is the fact that each of the four members of my family carry on the same practice with their children, usually reading at one meal a day.

It's true, we were never asked if we wanted to

do this; but then we were never asked if we wanted to do many other things which were good for us — like eating regular meals, taking baths, and going to school. I think the key is the way in which the teaching was accomplished. We knew this was an important Book in the lives of our parents. No sonorous, unnatural voice was used to bring God into family life. He was simply there, and each day we heard briefly what He had to say to us. The context was love, not law. And eighteen years of listening to God's truth and discussing and praying over it counts up!

I have never liked the words "family altar" or "family devotions." It's doubtless just a personal hang-up, but I think the words often conjur up a saccharin image of an open Bible in front of a bouquet of flowers, with a candle to one side and a family kneeling around this center. There's nothing wrong with this, but it's scary to some people. An altar isn't necessary since Jesus died for our sins, and devotion is what we should have toward God all day long, not just during a special time of the day. We prefer to call it family Bible reading, and we prefer to do it in a natural way at the end of a meal. As we talk about the day and its feelings, very often the passage we read together speaks to the issues involved. Prayer follows briefly and naturally.

The advantage of parents who are also studying the Scripture on their own is that they can refer to biblical truths quite naturally in daily conversation. Often a decision, a problem, an incident is recounted and these provide the very best teaching times if we know the Bible well enough to use it. No one else can be depended on to teach our children what they need to know about God.

AN IDEA THAT WORKS

When our son was small we began reading the Gospel of Mark aloud, including him in the family Bible reading. We read a short, narrative passage and then discussed it.

The father of our house proposed this plan: each person was to listen and in turn ask a question of the person on his left (or sometimes the person on the right; he made a game out of it). At first most of the questions were simply *questions of fact*: Where did Jesus go? What did the sick man do? But this involved listening well enough to make up the question and to answer one as well. Sometimes when there was company one's question got preempted and the person had to think up another.

The idea took hold quickly and we soon began interjecting *questions of interpretation*: Why did Jesus ask the man if he wanted to be healed? Why did Jesus tell the young man to sell his goods? Or *questions of application*: What can we learn about the way Jesus wants us to act?

The response was exciting as we dug into the Scripture with the three basic questions which comprise any good study: What does it say? (fact). What does it mean? (interpretation). What does it mean to me? (application). When Father introduced a two-part question, interest heightened even more. As time went on questions grew in depth of perception.

We have used this method over a period of years, and it has been a means of encouragement in simple Bible study, even to our household guests. It has encouraged listening and thinking about truth. We are pleased with the enthusiasm maintained by this method, as well as the perception of truth which has taken place. Truth demands interaction; it cannot be effectively poured over the head.

PRAYING TOGETHER

Out of such Bible reading comes a family's prayer life. We need to teach our family to pray over the content of Scripture, as well as over personal needs. Sentence prayers, which are not repetitious, encourage little people and big people alike, especially if they aren't prepared to make a long speech to God. We encourage family members to pray more than once, as we have our family conversation with God.

Praying as a family doesn't take the place of praying as husband and wife, however. The prayer level is different. Our children face many pressures of worldly ideas and behavior and we need to pray for them every day. We need to ask for open, obedient hearts. Husbands and wives need to bring themselves and their families before the throne of God's grace.

But a strange thing often happens: Husbands and wives feel self-conscious before God. If this is your case, why not discuss it openly and decide to do something about it. Maybe it's because you have too rigid a view of prayer. Maybe you think of prayer as a difficult speech made to God, who really hasn't accepted you anyway. Maybe you haven't let God inside your marriage with His ability to make you free. Maybe you've waited too long to begin. But all of these *maybes* can be taken care of by a decision to change the pattern which now exists.

It's very good just before falling asleep, perhaps to lie in each other's arms, to bring the children and your life together before God for His touch.

Loving God as a family is an adventure in His grace!

DISCUSSION QUESTIONS

1. Discuss the meaning of the parable of the king's treasure box. What benefits come from enjoying the treasure? How have you felt God's Word changing you?

2. What makes it difficult for Christians to study the Scripture consistently? (Get a list of honest answers here.)

What are the solutions to the problems discussed above?

3. What do you see in Israel's history which is repeated in our lives today?

4. In what ways are we responsible for the Word of God? (If we aren't responsible, who is?)

5. What is the advantage of being brought up in a Christian home?

6. What difficulties do you face in teaching your children about God (or in reading the Bible as husband and wife)?

If you engage in this practice, what pleasures do you enjoy?

7. Why do some people expect that strict discipline in instructing the family about spiritual truths will bring resentment?

In what ways can we be creative so that we don't need to hide behind that excuse?

8. Why does the chapter stress that no one else can do this for your children as effectively as you can?

9. Discuss the merits of the workable idea for family Bible reading presented in this chapter.

10. What creative steps can we take to improve our prayer life — as individuals? as couples? as families?

Who Knows
What You Are? 8

BEN AND GLORIA BENSON herd their three children out of the house and into the car every Sunday morning at 9:30. They usually wave a cheery hello to Fred and Janet in the next yard. Fred and Janet look up from their gardening and call a greeting in return.

The neighbors can almost set their clocks by the regularity of the Bensons' departure for church. If they feel at all guilty, they cover by joking about their religious neighbors.

Fred admits to Bob, who lives across the street, that he doesn't know Ben very well even after five years of being neighbors. He says Ben is a religious guy and probably wouldn't want to be invited over for a beer; and besides, he goes to church every other night, or at least it seems that way.

Bob's wife and Janet occasionally discuss the Bensons, too. When the neighbors get together in the morning for coffee, they usually don't invite Gloria. Religious people aren't very easy to be with, they say, and they might feel self-conscious about their conversation if she were there. Gloria doesn't mind not being invited because she really doesn't have time for this kind of thing.

Do any of the details of this story sound familiar to you? All over America genuine Christian families live in neighborhoods like this, go about their way of living, and are misunderstood because they don't communicate what they really are. After five years the Bensons' neighbors still think the choice is between being religious and not being religious. The Bensons choose to be religious. The neighbors don't. That's just the way it is.

We might think our behavior is a witness. But a witness to what? Often to being religious. The fact is that the average American is poorly taught in Christian beliefs. He may believe in God as a beautiful, transcendent concept, but his belief doesn't affect his life. When it comes to Jesus Christ, he may never have heard of His claims. Easter is like the first day of Spring to him, and he may get decked out and show up in church that day to capture enough religious feeling for the rest of the year.

He's heard of the resurrection, but considers it a lovely legend symbolic of life coming out of death — the bare brown earth springing alive with greenness. He doesn't know what Easter really means. And so when he sees someone who goes to church regularly and who doesn't have certain other habits, he simply classifies him as a pious Joe, a religious person, and that's that. No one has ever told him otherwise — not in a way that makes sense.

THE RELIGIOUS BARREL

I don't know about you, but I don't like being called religious. And yet that's what people will call us unless we begin to communicate about the Person we believe in who makes our lives different. Muslims are religious; so are Hindus. But I know Jesus Christ, and this is what my neighbors need to understand.

We may try to insert remarks about God or

Christ into our conversations, and this may open the door for further discussions; but unless further discussions ensue, we end up in the old "religious barrel" along with the others who have queer beliefs. And let's not delude ourselves into thinking that is enough.

I remember hearing the physical education instructor in our high school report to the other teachers in the staff lounge that Mary Richards was being excused from physical education on the days when the class did social dancing. The instructor had asked her why, and Mary had replied, "Because I don't believe Jesus wants me to."

The instructor hooted over such "religious nuts" and had no understanding whatever of why Mary was concerned about Jesus. Frankly, she thought Mary was using Jesus as an excuse because she was overweight and clumsy on her feet. I went to bat for Mary and tried to explain her conviction. But it wasn't easy. Perhaps it would have been easier if Mary had been radiating Christ in other areas of her life. Maybe this was all she could do to be true to her convictions, but somehow I felt Christ was misrepresented and I longed for the teacher to understand about Him.

Obviously, people aren't always going to understand, even when we try our best. But let's try to communicate so that others won't think we're peculiar in the wrong sense of that word. They ought to know what we are and why.

OUR ATTITUDE AND OUR MESSAGE

Our attitudes will make all the difference in the area of genuine communication. If we come on in conversation sounding like we care more about truth than people, we'll not get very far. If we communicate "my church" instead of Jesus Christ, we will only widen the gap. If we invite our neighbors to a special meeting at church, but have little time for them otherwise, we might as well not waste our time.

People want to be liked for who they are. Sometimes we give the impression we care about their soul, not their person. Other times we act as though the person needs to become more like us so they will be fit to hear the message. Reading the life of Jesus Christ and observing His concern for the total person should jolt us out of such hazards. Remember how He had time for the blind man, even though the crowds thought someone as important as Jesus wouldn't want to bother about a beggar? Jesus even gave him the dignity of making his own request for sight. And then there was that sinner Zacchaeus whom Jesus called by name because He wanted to visit in his house with him.

Remember our message is Jesus Christ. The good news is that Jesus loves sinners and came to redeem them. A man can know God because of Jesus Christ. These truths ought to excite us enough to move us out of our tight circles of security into our neighborhoods to communicate.

LEARNING TO COMMUNICATE

How can we communicate with our friends and neighbors instead of just talking religion at them? Easy success formulas for the Christian life aren't available, but just being aware of the problem and wanting to change it is a very hopeful beginning. Learning a method, memorizing verses — all the gimmicks in the world have only limited value. You have to begin by caring enough to know another person.

We've got all the plus factors on our side. We know God through Jesus Christ. We have the Holy Spirit indwelling us and helping us. First of all, then, the initiative is ours. We take God's attitude in this. He came to communicate to us. The incarnation is a tremendous fact!

Secondly, we can ask the Holy Spirit to help us to be natural. Instead of our blood pressure rising 50 points because we're going to inject our bit about God into the conversation, let's ask God to make us natural in speaking about Him. That may take a while, but it is no excuse to stop trying or asking God to help us.

Often we are so worried about "dumping our load" of truth that we only make matters worse. We fail to listen to what the other person is saying and to find out where he is in his thinking. We do all the talking.

Learn to ask questions. Listen. Earn the right to finally ask, "What do you believe about God?" Build a bridge of friendship so you can begin to communicate. But don't let the bridge-building take so long that he moves away before he's heard what you want to tell him.

When a woman in our town began coming to Bible study in one of the neighbor's homes, she avoided me like the plague because she was scared of me. I often led the study; I was religious. She felt her life made her otherwise. God put it in my heart to spend extra time with her so she could see I was an ordinary person, but one who knew God. We took a physical fitness class together; we laughed together, stopped off for a cup of coffee and conversation. One day she said one of the nicest things anyone can say about another person. She said, "You know, before I knew you I thought you were just another religious person. But now I see that you're a believer in Jesus Christ." By building friendships we convey our common humanity in refreshing ways and we communicate that God *loves* people.

Let's recap what we've been discovering: (1) take the initiative; (2) ask God to make us natural in conversation; (3) build a bridge of friendship so we can earn the right to share our faith in Jesus Christ.

Taking these steps could result in inviting the neighbor over for a cup of coffee and a conversation which could lead to reading the Bible together. Neighborhood Bible studies are one of the best ways to communicate the truth about Jesus Christ because the Bible speaks with more authority than we can. Whatever we do, God can make us creative in our outreach.

It's not enough to withdraw and simply look religious. We've got to establish contact with our neighbors. But if we go and visit with them, they must know what we are. We cannot be silent.

The world is troubled and confused. People are looking for someone who knows the way. We have found the One who *is* the Way. How dreadful for us will be the day of judgment if we have to admit, "Lord, I lived next door to them for five years, but I never helped them to understand."

DISCUSSION QUESTIONS

1. What do your neighbors observe about you from watching the life-style of your family?

2. How much of the Christian message is communicated to them by their observations?

3. What do you think your neighbors believe about God or about Jesus Christ?

4. What do they think a Christian is?

How did they receive whatever ideas they hold?

(If you have no contributions to make in the discussion of questions 3 and 4, what might this show about you?)

5. Why are we often so slow to speak of our faith to others?

What does the example of the incarnation teach us about taking the initiative?

6. Think through the gradual stages of what your friends and neighbors can begin to understand about you. What is one of the first things you want them to notice? Why? What progression do you want your witness to make?

7. In what sense ought we to be a "peculiar" people? Should this necessarily be offensive to non-Christians?

8. How can children be an aid to our witness in a neighborhood? What cautions should be taken?

9. From the preceding chapter, share as a group the ideas which strike home most effectively as you consider your witness as a family.

10. If you are an apartment dweller, what special problems affect your witness?

9 A Summary Discussion

A SUMMARY DISCUSSION

The preceding chapters have provided a look at the facets of family life. If the group agrees that a recap discussion would be profitable, several approaches to summarizing could be used. Plan your time carefully for you will not be able to use all of the ideas given below.

(1) Assign eight people to give a brief summary of the key ideas of each chapter.

(2) Review by choosing a key question from each chapter for discussion.

(3) Use the questions below, supplementing them with others which arise out of the discussion. Do not be content with easy answers.

    a. Summarize the salient points of this book by describing the kind of family life here proposed.

    b. Define the quality of relationship between various family members discussed in this book. How would these affect our view of ourselves and free us in relating to others?

c. Define individual responsibilities within the family. How do these affect the lives of individual family members?

d. Discuss the impact of this kind of family life as a witness to others.

(4) Conclude with a time of group prayer, encouraging members to pray briefly and honestly.

NOTES

NOTES

NOTES

NOTES

NOTES

NOTES

NOTES